AMAZING AUTO RACING RECORDS

BY BRIAN HOWELL

Published by The Child's World®
1980 Lookout Drive • Mankato, MN 56003-1705
800-599-READ • www.childsworld.com

Acknowledgments
The Child's World®: Mary Berendes, Publishing Director
The Design Lab: Design
Amnet: Production
Red Line Editorial: Editorial direction

Design Element: Tom Grill/Shutterstock Images

Photographs ©: Walter G Arce/Shutterstock Images,
Cover, 7, 9; Library of Congress, 5; AP Images, 11;
Chris O'Meara/AP Images, 13; Bob Daugherty/AP
Images, 15; Paul Beaty/AP Images, 17; Bettmann/Corbis/
AP Images, 19, 27; David Acosta Allely/Shutterstock
Images, 21; Steve Kohls/AP Images, 23; The Indianapolis
Star/Greg Griffo/AP Images, 25; David Vincent/AP
Images, 29.

ISBN 9781614734000
LCCN 2012946495

Printed in the United States of America
Mankato, MN
November, 2012
PA02146

Disclaimer: The information in this book is current
through the 2011 NASCAR season.

ABOUT THE AUTHOR

Brian Howell is a freelance writer from Denver, Colorado. He has been a sports journalist for nearly 20 years, writing about high school, college, and professional sports. He has also written books about sports and history.

TABLE OF CONTENTS

ONE

THE SPORT OF AUTO RACING

For almost as long as there have been automobiles, people have raced them against each other.
The first organized long-distance race was held in 1895. It took place in France, running from Paris to Bordeaux. The distance was 732 miles (1,178 km). The winner had an average speed of just 15 miles per hour (mph) (24.15 kmh). Since this first race, the urge to be faster than everyone else has produced dozens of great racing champions.

One of the best champions of all time is Jimmie Johnson. As hard as they tried, the other National Association of Stock Car Racing (NASCAR) drivers couldn't beat Johnson. For five years in a row, Johnson was the king of NASCAR. From 2006 to 2010, he won every Cup Series championship. That **streak** is one of the most amazing records in auto racing.

FIRST RACE ON A CLOSED CIRCUIT

On May 1, 1898, the first closed-circuit road race was held on the Course de Périgueux in France. Each lap on the circuit had a distance of 90 miles (145 km).

People watch a 1900 auto race in Long Island, New York.

Winning five championships in a row does not happen very often in sports. It had never happened in the NASCAR Cup Series, which is a championship based on points. Prior to 2006, the longest winning streak in Cup Series history came from Cale Yarborough. He won three in a row from 1976 to 1978.

To win his fifth Cup Series, Johnson had to come from behind in the final race of the year. He finished in second place, which was good enough to give him the points championship yet again. During his five-year reign at the top, Johnson won 35 races. It was his five Cup Series season championships in a row, however, that was Johnson's greatest act.

EARNHARDT GOES BACK-TO-BACK THREE TIMES

Through 2011, there were ten drivers who won back-to-back Cup Series championships. Of those ten, Dale Earnhardt Sr. was the only driver to win back-to-back titles on three different occasions (1986–87, 1990–91, and 1993–94). Richard Petty was the only other driver to do it twice (1971–72 and 1974–75).

NASCAR'S FIRST $8 MILLION MAN

In 2006, when Jimmie Johnson won his first Cup Series title, he brought home a record $8.9 million in earnings. In fact, during his five-year streak of titles, Johnson won at least $7.2 million each year—totaling $38.5 million. In 2011, Carl Edwards won $8.5 million, joining Johnson as the only drivers to top $8 million in a season.

Jimmie Johnson celebrates after winning the NSCS Pepsi 500 on October 11, 2009.

AMAZING STOCK CAR RECORDS

Richard Petty was born into a racing family. In fact, his father, Lee, was one of the greatest NASCAR drivers ever. Petty wound up **surpassing** his father. He was so good that he earned the nickname "The King."

Petty set three records that may never be broken. In 1967, he set the record for most wins in a season (27) and for most wins in a row (10). Petty also had 200 career Cup Series victories. That is 95 more than any other driver in history.

MOST NASCAR CUP SERIES CHAMPIONSHIPS

Richard Petty: 7	**David Pearson:** 3
Dale Earnhardt Sr.: 7	**Cale Yarborough:** 3
Jimmie Johnson*: 5	**Darrell Waltrip:** 3
Jeff Gordon*: 4	**Tony Stewart*:** 3
Lee Petty: 3	

*Active as of 2012

MOST CUP SERIES WINS IN NASCAR

DRIVER	CAREER WINS
Richard Petty	**200**
David Pearson	**105**
Jeff Gordon*	**85**
Bobby Allison	**84**
Darrell Waltrip	**84**

*Active as of 2012

Richard Petty sits at the wheel on July 4, 2009, during a ceremony honoring the 25th anniversary of his 200th win in 1984.

ELLIOTT SETS SPEED RECORD

Talladega Superspeedway has had some amazing events in racing history. One of the greatest was on April 30, 1987. That's when Bill Elliott set a NASCAR speed record. He hit 212.089 mph (341.324 kmh) while qualifying for that weekend's race. But, a big crash in that race injured fans.

After that crash, NASCAR started using **restrictor plates** to slow cars down. Restrictor plates reduce the power made by motors. Slowing cars down aims to make racing safer for drivers and fans. Because of the plates, Elliott's record might last forever. Elliott had 44 wins and 175 top-five finishes in his amazing career.

GANT'S STREAK

In 1991, 51-year-old "Handsome Harry" Gant had one of the most amazing months in NASCAR history. During a three-week span, from September 1 to September 22, Gant won six **consecutive** races. That included four Cup Series wins and two lower-level series wins. Gant earned the nickname "Mr. September." But he lost by just 1.5 seconds the following week.

OLDEST DRIVERS TO START CUP SERIES RACES

DRIVER	AGE	YEAR
Hershel McGriff	65	1993
Jim Fitzgerald	65	1987
Morgan Shepherd	64	2006
Geoff Bodine	62	2011
Dave Marcis	61	2002
Dick Trickle	60	2002

Bill Elliott removes his helmet after setting his speed record in 1987.

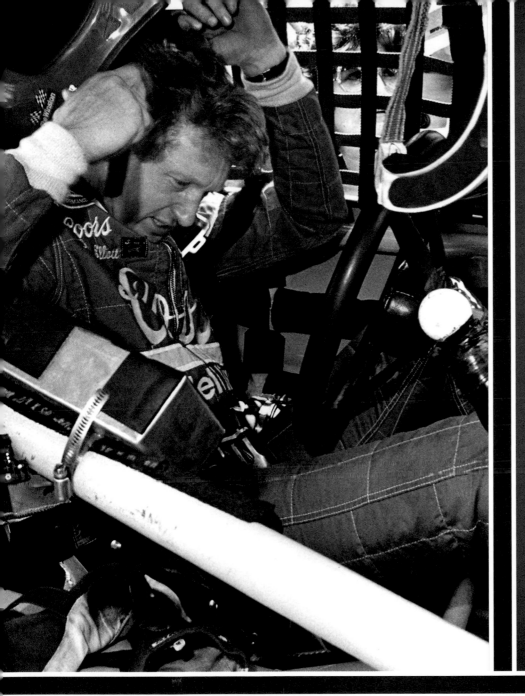

THE YOUNGEST WINNER

The 2009 Sprint Cup season was a great one for 19-year-old Joey Logano. That year, he became the only teenager to win a Sprint Cup race. He won the Lenox Industrial Tools 301, despite leading just ten of the 273 laps. With seven top-ten finishes on the season, Logano also became the youngest winner of the Rookie of the Year award.

YOUNGEST DRIVER IN NASCAR

NASCAR history was made at Altamont-Schenectady Fairgrounds in New York on August 1, 1951. Tommie Elliott became the youngest driver to ever start a NASCAR race. He was 15 years, 7 months, and 5 days old at the time of the race. Elliott finished in fifteenth place. Through 2011, he was still the only driver younger than 17 to compete.

TRIUMPH AND TRAGEDY AT DAYTONA

One of the most beloved drivers in auto racing was Dale Earnhardt Sr. Famous for driving the No. 3 car, "The Intimidator" won 76 Cup Series races and seven series titles. However, the Daytona 500 proved to be a difficult race for Earnhardt. In 1998, Earnhardt broke through and won his first Daytona 500 on his twentieth try. No driver in history has raced that many times before winning his first Daytona 500.

Three years later, tragedy occurred at the 2001 Daytona 500. On the final lap, Earnhardt's car tangled with another and then crashed into the wall. The injuries he suffered were very severe. He died later that afternoon. Michael Waltrip was the winner, while Earnhardt's son, Dale Earnhardt Jr., was second. Earnhardt Sr. was in third place nearing into the final lap.

In 2004, Earnhardt Jr. won the Daytona 500. The Earnhardts are one of three father-son duos to both win the Daytona 500. Lee Petty and Richard Petty and Bobby Allison and Davey Allison are the others.

CLOSEST FINISHES IN CUP SERIES RACES

1. Ricky Craven won by 0.002 seconds in 2003 at the Carolina Dodge Dealers 400.
(tie) Jimmie Johnson won by 0.002 seconds in 2011 at the Aaron's 499.
3. Dale Earnhardt Sr. won by 0.005 seconds in 1993 at the DieHard 500.
(tie) Jamie McMurray won by 0.005 seconds in 2007 at the Pepsi 400.
5. Kevin Harvick won by 0.006 seconds in 2001 at the Cracker Barrel 500.

THE BIG ONE

Talladega Superspeedway in Alabama is one of the most famous racetracks in NASCAR. It has been the home to several great moments and notorious crashes. In 2005, Talladega had one of the biggest crashes in NASCAR history. During the Aaron's 499, 28 cars were involved in a massive crash. Somehow, nobody was seriously injured.

After winning the Daytona 500 in 1998, Dale Earnhardt Sr. holds up his trophy.

MOST DAYTONA 500 VICTORIES

DRIVER	WINS
Richard Petty	7
Cale Yarborough	4
Bobby Allison	3
Dale Jarrett	3
Jeff Gordon*	3

*Active as of 2012

THREE

AMAZING OPEN-WHEEL RECORDS

A. J. Foyt was the first driver to win the Indianapolis 500 four times. He also won more IndyCar races than any other driver. One of his greatest feats, however, was winning three different major events. Foyt is the only driver in history to win the Indianapolis 500, NASCAR's Daytona 500, and the 24 Hours of Le Mans. It was impressive because of the differences in all the races. IndyCar racing is done with open-wheel cars, which generally seat just one person and are built for racing. NASCAR uses stock cars, which look more like regular street cars. The Le Mans race is one of racing's greatest **endurance** tests. Foyt teamed with Dan Gurney to win the 1967 24-hour race. That was the only time in the history of the event, which began in 1923, that an all-American team won.

MOST INDYCAR WINS (CAREER)

1. A. J. Foyt: 67
2. Mario Andretti: 52
3. Michael Andretti: 42
4. Al Unser: 39
5. Bobby Unser: 35

A. J. Foyt prepares for the Indianapolis 500 in May 1965.

CASTRONEVES ROARS TO WIN

Before every race, drivers compete for the pole position. This puts the driver in front of the pack to start the race. The drivers in the back have a tough time moving up and getting a win. In 2008, however, Helio Castroneves came from the back to win a race at the Chicagoland Speedway. Castroneves started in the twenty-eighth position. That is the lowest starting position of any race winner in IndyCar history.

DRIVERS WITH AT LEAST THREE INDIANAPOLIS 500 WINS

DRIVER	WINS
A. J. Foyt	4
Al Unser	4
Rick Mears	4
Louis Meyer	3
Wilbur Shaw	3
Mauri Rose	3
Johnny Rutherford	3
Bobby Unser	3
Helio Castroneves*	3
Dario Franchitti*	3

*Active as of 2012

Helio Castroneves leads the pack during a race at Chicagoland Speedway on September 7, 2008.

UNSER FAMILY LEADS PACK

Several families have famous names in auto racing: Allison, Andretti, Bodine, Busch, Earnhardt, Rahal, and Waltrip. But, perhaps no family is as connected to IndyCar racing as the Unser family. Together, Unser family members won 110 IndyCar races. In fact, three members of the family rank among the top six winners in IndyCar history. Al Unser won 39 races, while his brother Bobby won 35. Al Unser Jr. won 34 races. Louis Unser won two races. As a group, the family won the Indianapolis 500 nine times.

PATRICK FINISHES THIRD

Danica Patrick was not the first female to race at the Indianapolis 500, but she's been the most successful. In 2005, Patrick became the first female to ever lead the race. She held the lead for 19 laps. In 2009, Patrick finished third at the Indianapolis 500. That is the best finish ever for a female driver.

FAMILIES WITH MOST INDYCAR SERIES WINS*

1. Unser family: 110 wins
2. Andretti family: 97 wins
3. Rahal family: 25 wins
4. Fittipaldi family: 24 wins

*Only families with at least 2 different winners are listed. These include IndyCar races before the formal series started in 1996.

Al Unser raises three fingers after his third Indianapolis 500 win in 1978.

SCHUMACHER RULES F1

Formula 1 (F1) racing is popular around the world. The F1 Series features fast cars, and its best drivers are known worldwide. One of the best drivers in F1 has been Michael Schumacher. He holds several F1 records, including 91 career wins. That is 40 more than any other driver. Driving for car manufacturer Ferrari, he also won seven season championships, including five in a row from 2000 to 2004.

THE YOUNGEST OPEN-WHEEL RACER

On April 18, 2004, Nelson Philippe made open-wheel racing history. At 17 years, 8 months, and 25 days old, Philippe became the youngest racer in open-wheel history when he competed in the Champ Car World Series. In fact, he is the only racer under 18 years old ever to compete.

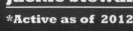

MOST WINS IN F1 (CAREER)

DRIVER	WINS
Michael Schumacher*	91
Alain Prost	51
Ayrton Senna	41
Nigel Mansell	31
Fernando Alonso*	27
Jackie Stewart	27

*Active as of 2012

YOUNGEST F1 RACE WINNERS

1. **Sebastian Vettel: 21 years and 73 days in 2008**
2. **Fernando Alonso: 22 years and 26 days in 2003**
3. **Troy Ruttman: 22 years and 80 days in 1952**

Michael Schumacher drives his F1 car during a training session in Spain on October 11, 2006.

OTHER AMAZING AUTO RACING RECORDS

It is common for drivers to pass the racing tradition on to their sons. Auto racing history is full of fathers and sons who have driven, and succeeded, in different areas of auto racing. It's not often, however, that a man's daughters pick up the sport.

John Force had 134 career wins in drag racing. He is also the only driver to win as many as 100 races in the National Hot Rod Association (NHRA). Force won 15 season championships, including one in 2010 when he was 61 years old.

SCHUMACHER HITS 337

On August 13, 2005, Tony Schumacher recorded the fastest run in the history of drag racing. In Brainerd, Minnesota, Schumacher's Top Fuel car reached an amazing 337.58 mph (543.28 kmh)! He also has the most career wins in Top Fuel, with 68.

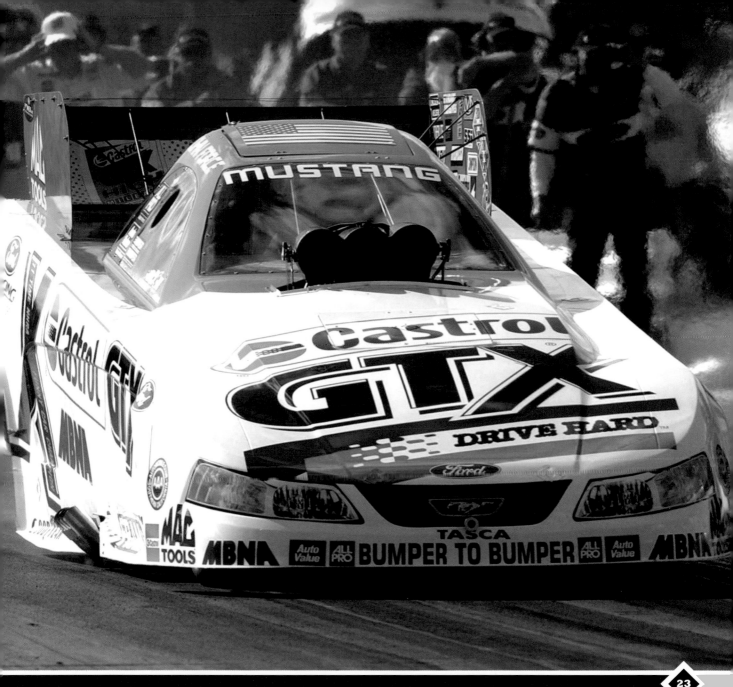

John Force powers his Ford Mustang funny car during qualifying for the NHRA Rugged Liner Nationals at Brainerd International Raceway in 2002.

Force passed on his love for drag racing to his daughters. Ashley, Courtney, and Brittany have all become **accomplished** dragsters like their father. Ashley won four NHRA events from 2007 to 2010. Courtney began her pro career in 2012. Brittany also had plenty of racing experience behind the wheel.

MOST NHRA WINS (CAREER)

DRIVER	WINS
John Force*	134
Warren Johnson*	97
Frank Manzo*	96
Bob Glidden	85
David Rampy*	80

*Active as of 2012

25

TOP SPEEDS IN NHRA HISTORY
1. Tony Schumacher: 337.58 mph (543.28 kmh)
2. Doug Kalitta: 335.57 mph (540.05 kmh)
3. Hillary Will: 334.65 mph (538.57 kmh)
4. Mike Ashley: 334.32 mph (538.04 kmh)
5. J. R. Todd: 334.24 mph (537.91 kmh)

Ashley Force holds up her trophy after her funny car win at the Mac Tools U.S. Nationals at O'Reilly Raceway Park in 2009.

PRUDHOMME NEARLY UNBEATABLE

In 1976, funny car driver Don Prudhomme had one of the most amazing seasons in history. The legendary driver set an NHRA record with seven wins. He had five that season and two in 1975. Prudhomme won the season championship for the second year in a row. In fact, he won four championships in a row from 1975 to 1978.

MOLDOVAN KEPT GOING AND GOING

Romanian driver Laurentiu Moldovan had the longest career of any auto racing driver in history. He raced rally cars and F1 cars. Moldovon's career began on July 7, 1968, at the age of 35. His career lasted 39 years and 364 days. Moldovan's career ended in tragedy on July 6, 2008. In his final race, he got into his first-ever accident during the national championships in Romania. Moldovan died as a result of the accident.

RACING AT 90

On August 3, 2003, Jeannie Reiman competed in the Canadian Vintage Modified's ten-lap Powder Puff race in Stroud, Ontario, Canada. Reiman became the oldest female race car driver that day. She competed at the age of 90 years and 106 days.

Don Prudhomme smiles from his car in 1970.

TEST OF ENDURANCE

The 24 Hours of Le Mans may be the most difficult event in auto racing. The annual race is held on a track in Le Mans, France. In 2010, a team of drivers for Audi set an impressive distance record. Mike Rockenfeller, Timo Bernhard, and Romain Dumas teamed up to complete 397 laps in their Audi R15. Those 397 laps covered a whopping 3,362.1 miles (5,410.8 km)—all in 24 hours! The previous record was set in 1971. That year Helmut Marko and Gijs van Lennep drove their Porsche 917K for 3,315.2 miles (5,335.3 km).

28 LARGEST AVERAGE ATTENDANCE

EVENT	RACETRACK	FANS
Indianapolis 500	Indianapolis Motor Speedway in Indiana	400,000
NASCAR Brickyard 400	Indianapolis Motor Speedway in Indiana	257,000
24 Hours Nürburgring	Nürburgring in Germany	200,000
Daytona 500	Daytona International Speedway in Florida	185,000

NO. 1 NOT SO LUCKY

Generally, the number one is associated with being the best. In NASCAR history, however, that isn't the case. In the three NASCAR series (Sprint Cup, Nationwide, and Truck) there has been only one driver with the No. 1 car that won a series championship. That honor went to Ted Musgrave, who won in 2005.

Audi teammates Mike Rockenfeller, Romain Dumas, and Timo Bernhard hold up their trophies after winning the 24 Hours of Le Mans race in 2010.

GLOSSARY

accomplished (uh-KOM-plishd): An accomplished driver has driven successfully in races. Dale Earnhardt Sr. was an accomplished racer.

consecutive (kuhn-SEK-yuh-tiv): Something that is consecutive happens one after the other. Harry Gant won six consecutive races in 1991.

notorious (noh-TOR-ee-uhss): If something is notorious, it is well known for something bad. Talladega Superspeedway has had some notorious crashes.

restrictor plates (ri-STRIKT-uhr PLAYTZ): Restrictor plates are put in a car's engine to limit the power of the car and slow it down. After 1987, NASCAR started using restrictor plates at its races.

streak (STREEK): A streak is an unbroken series of events. Jimmie Johnson had a streak of five straight Cup Series championships from 2006 to 2010.

surpassing (sur-PASS-ing): Surpassing is doing better than another person's record or career. Richard Petty ended up surpassing his father's racing career.

LEARN MORE

Books

Christopher, Matt. *Great Moments in American Auto Racing.*
New York: Little, Brown and Co., 2011.

Dooling, Michael. *The Great Horse-less Carriage Race.*
New York: Holiday House, 2002.

Ford, Michael. *Dale Earnhardt, Jr.* New York:
Gareth Stevens, 2011.

Roberts, Angela. *NASCAR's Greatest Drivers.* New York:
Random House, 2009.

Web Sites

Visit our Web site for links about auto racing records:
childsworld.com/links

Note to Parents, Teachers, and Librarians:
We routinely verify our Web links to make sure they are safe and
active sites. So encourage your readers to check them out!

INDEX